Spirital

A Real Soul Evolution Experience

Lark Lauren

Spirital - A Real Soul Evolution Experience

Spirital, Volume 1

Lark Lauren

Published by Lark Lauren, 2023.

While every precaution has been taken in the preparation of this book, the publisher assumes no responsibility for errors or omissions, or for damages resulting from the use of the information contained herein.

SPIRITAL - A REAL SOUL EVOLUTION EXPERIENCE

First edition. January 16, 2023.

Copyright © 2023 Lark Lauren.

ISBN: 979-8215120507

Written by Lark Lauren.

Also by Lark Lauren

Spirital

Spirital - A Real Soul Evolution Experience

Spirital - Making Sense

Spirital - The Symphony of Coming Home

Spirital - A Real Soul Evolution Experience and Making Sense

Table of Contents

To My Wonderful Wife and Son that give me immense joy,
hope, and fantastic support every day.

To My Extended Family that is close in mind and spirit.

To My Friends that are consistently in contact helping and
encouraging me.

... and not lastly ...

To the Great Team of Professionals working passionately
towards my recovery.

This book is also dedicated to All Human Beings who feel that
Love is the answer, and that the gentle, genuine, considerate,
and compassionate interaction are the basis of our communities.

Printed in the United States of America

Disclaimer

This book describes the experiences of the author. The events and interpretations are described from his perspective. This book content does not constitute advice of any kind and it should be taken as information only, offering just a different and unique perspective.

The author is not responsible for effects or consequences readers have or allegedly might have by reading this book. The information provided in this book does not constitute medical advice and is not a substitute for conventional medical assistance or treatment.

Introduction

Spirital is not a misspelling. It is a name that was suggested for this project during a deep meditation.

A very logical mind, Lark Lauren suffered a traumatic event. He is describing his path to awakening after this event which made him realize there is something else there, beyond the obvious. Follow the inspiring journey that opens him to the truth and puts him on the path of achieving the ultimate Joy.

Spirital - A Real Soul Evolution Experience is exploring concepts, feelings, realizations, and sensations from a practical perspective, the exact way that Lark experienced them at the time as well as their relation to the modern society and environment.

Lark Lauren undergoes a transformation and starts paying attention to the spiritual world, to what is around us, and to what we take for granted. During the story, the narration changes from the third person to the first person showing the transformation and evolution from the old to the new.

Lark gets us thinking beyond the mainstream and experiencing the deep connection we have with the Universe.

This is a real soul evolution story.

After The Traumatic Event

In the Now he felt the gentle breeze and warmth that reminded him of his childhood walks under the moon, behind the linden trees. It has been several years from this event and his outlook about life changed so much from the first flashlight of hope when he was in the hospital. After nights of fear, worries and pain, he saw himself lying on the beach, under the sun. Still, he realized that he was just lying on a hospital bed, but it was like he was levitating now. Everything started to look easy out of the sudden. A bright yellow, almost orange light, the light of life was shining upon him. At that moment he understood that all will be ok and he will get better and recover. He understood that God's light was guiding him, and he felt it radiating the love of the family and friends and of the whole Universe on his cheeks. It was his first experience of the supranatural.

It was incredible to him that in a world that seemed cold, indifferent, and superficial, he was covered in so much love and compassion. God and Love were real after all. The society did not destroy it all. Maybe the world was not in fact indifferent, but just seemed that way from afar. Discovering these deeper connections and meanings was refreshing. We are all connected after all. We are One.

The Ego

Months after the event, when he read and listened to Eckhart Tolle and other masters like Sadhguru, Brian Scott, RJ Spina, he realized that at that moment, during and immediately after the event, he was living in the genuine Now. His mind was not judging anymore. It has been taken over by something higher, being the higher self, the Source, or the subconscious mind. Suddenly, all around seemed helpful, transmitting love and compassion. The limiting program, the Ego, was conquered and subsided to exist. This Ego always judging, "thinking" and battling something may be a source of all our ignorance and evil. You can see it everywhere. We are running an addiction program in our minds. We use our minds inadequately by trying to reason everything through the lenses of the past, trying to predict our future and consistently worrying. The Ego, this judging voice that we are apparently addicted to, knows that it is not helpful and knows that it cannot help you. It shuts down in the moments of crisis. It shuts down as RJ Spina says when you are asking it if this is You - "Is this voice in my head me? Is this I? After you ask yourself this question, you may be surprised that the voice does not respond back anymore. Is like it has been caught. So, that is obviously not you but so many people are still identifying with it, thinking that the Ego is them, it is who they are. That judging, sometimes rude "entity" filling your head every minute of the day is not you. It is just an automatic addictive program that we started to be taking over by as soon as we started reading, started learning, and were programmed to function in the society.

Meditation

The insanity is continuing, amplified by the fact that we are now indoctrinated daily through what can be called "tunnel vision" devices - our smartphones, tablets, computers, etc. These are all just devices to induce fear, amplify our egos and keep us captive to the judging voice, keep us inside the limiting program created in our head. It is like we were implemented this program to be able to be controlled and manipulated. But we are just pure, perfect joy at our core. I started to experience more of that joy later when I was starting meditating. Some think that meditating is just a result of listening or watching a mesmerizing recording, but in the months to follow I learned that those can only be a catalyst.

For him, meditating is just the effortless connection with the inner self. He was fascinated by the story of the little Buddha which at early age, being left alone, discovers that following his breath gives him peace and breaks the loop of always thinking about something and that this brought him an immense joy. He has discovered that we are just a way for the Divine to experience the physical world. This energy flowing through us, continuously communicating is what some call God, the Universe, or the Field. The essence of life are experiences. It is the search for that joy through experiences that has the most impact on us. We learn through these experiences and through them we are getting closer to our core, the Divine.

Feeling The Joy

He started feeling the need to go outside and experience Nature, the Universe. After lying in bed for weeks, his soul was craving energetical outdoor exposure, just many times being saddened by the fact that it was either too dangerous for him to go, it was raining or there was no-one available to take him. Before the pandemic hit, which cause the hospital to not allow visitors anymore, his wife would take him, and it was beautiful. Even now, it brings tears of joy into his eyes. These tears are generated by the realization of knowing that someone is genuinely loving you and knowing instinctively what you need. His wife is a wonderful human being and has been and is a fantastic and beautiful part of him and his recovery. This feeling of joy has been amplified when his wife was driving him home after completing his rehabilitation program at the hospital. Seating in the car, feeling loved and looking at the majesty of Nature brought him so much joy. The Nature and the joy of participating in it was something he never paid very close attention to before. It was the beautiful feeling of joy created by experiencing nature. This made him realize that getting out of the house, into nature, just by walking or driving around brings a subliminal sentiment of joy that is very important for our being. Just go out, experience nature in any way you can. It will fuel your inner being, your beautiful Self.

Nature Wonder

The experience of nature's energy did not stop here. He would sit in the backyard, and he was surprised to realize that he noticed amplified sounds and images of the life around him, from the small seeds falling out of gumtree fruits under which his bench was, to the beating of the wings of birds and insects, to the leaves falling all around him. He realized that he was still living in the Now at times. These moments were mostly generated by experiencing nature. He was sitting on the bench under the tree once and looking straight ahead. It was autumn. Leaves were falling. He decided instinctively to watch couple of leaves falling from up high all the way down to the ground. Doing this for several minutes was beautiful. It was like the time has stopped. He changed his focus from the individual leaves and started looking at the big picture. Then it was when all the joy broke loose. He was looking now to a grand landscape with trees, a lake, grass, and the sky. His house backyard opens in a park. What was surprising and brought him the ultimate joy was that looking at the big picture, he was now noticing all the leaves around him falling at once everywhere. It was a beautiful and serene experience. He was even seeing the leaves of the trees near the houses across the park falling all at once. It was a multiplied joy experience.

Try the same thing for yourself. You may experience the beauty of nature and you may surprise yourself.

Many times, we lose sight of the big picture, crunched over our "tunnel vision" devices, like our cell phones, tablets or computers and only seeing fabricated reality. We miss the big picture, the beauty and energy of nature, we get too much concentrated on, many times, "nasty" details, and negative information. The news and Internet outlets know that we are inclined to pay more attention to shocking or negative news, and they are consistently pumping these. Try to be selective, take your attention away from the noise to experience the joyful being of You.

The Metaphysical

Dictating this, talking about my experiences, it is not even feeling like writing. It all feels effortless. It is coming from my inner being, the mind is little involved, it all seems to come automatically and easy and this only happens in the moments of "inspiration". It may be something that some may call so easily a "channeling". I see these moments coming to me more often. Writing about these, I realized that it brings me much joy. To You, the Being that is reading this, I hope you may find something here to further elevate and enlighten you. Many of us are in a need of an awakening to discover who we truly are, to get to our essence. Sending Love, good thoughts, and ultimate Joy, to you my dear One. Blessings!

One of the days, communication came to me emphasizing the concept that every incarnation of every being is an experience that "God" transposes through you. God is for me a personification, the energy of life. This energy is within you, plays with the Universe and wants to experience it all. You are the energy of life experiencing the physical raum. You are the Universe; you are that energy, and every being is. We are all a part of God. Did you ever watch yourself in the mirror and asked the question "Who are You?". The answer may never come back to you because you just Are. It is more like "I am who I am". If you answered Me and used a gesture to show towards your chest, it will say it all to you. You are not your brain, you are not your thoughts, you are this divine Self that resides deep inside. Anything you put after "I am", trying to characterize you, can only be the result of the thinking, of the egoic mind expression. Love yourself because "You just Are".

What resonate with your being may not resonate with mine. My convictions may not resonate with others. We are still trying to influence others through our beliefs. It has been the case for centuries and it continues until this moment.

If you take a moment to just experience the Now, the moment of freeing your mind of any beliefs, memories, and worries, you might experience your true essence.

Meditating

Since I did a Hebrew meditation guided by Brian Scott, I realized that old Hebrew words, names and expressions have a great influence and impression on my being. For some reason, they feel serene and powerful at the same time, they feel at home and peaceful, deep, and have a vibration to them - words like Adonai, Yahweh, Yahshua, Torah, Zorah, Katosh. These old Hebrew words/names seem to have power, an energy and a vibration embedded in them. That is why maybe some music like that of Nathaniel Bassey in the song Adonai, resonates with me so deeply. During that guided Hebrew meditation, I transcended in what seemed to be an outer space, away from my body and experienced multiple colors in what it seemed to be the inner mind since my eyes were closed. The colors changed in what it seemed to be a specific rhythm. They will switch from yellow to orange, red, green, blue, but what stayed with me was the deep purple which seemed to have been coming at the end of each cycle. I do not remember the exact succession of the colors, but I certainly remember the colors changing and always ending with that deep, beautiful purple. It was a wonderful experience, similar with my experience of the supranatural in the hospital, but much more enhanced. By this time, I was successfully practicing meditation almost daily, by the guidance of Brian Scott, Sadhguru, and Andy from Headspace.

I started to meditate at the recommendation of friends and family. My therapist also recommended it to alleviate pain. My therapist is a kind human being and she recommended me to listen to Headspace, the meditation iPhone app. I am so grateful for her recommendation. So, I was listening to Andy on Headspace which was guiding me in meditation for different purposes. The whole experience was enlightening. First, I wanted to do this to alleviate my physical pain. Using Andy's techniques, I was surprised that, in time, I was able to diffuse the intense pain and not identify with it anymore, especially during the physical therapy sessions. This was a fantastic discovery and propelled me to a different level, to understand more of how our mind works and what is possible. It proved to me that it was something more there, something to be explored and discovered. A great friend also recommended to listen to Brian Scott, Aaron Abke, and others. This is how I started to make sense of the consciousness evolution process.

Habits and The Subconscious

Does this happen to you? Especially in the morning but also at random moments throughout the day, the rhythm of a song plays in your mind. It happens to me sometimes. It could be something that I listened the day before. This is the subconscious mind playing a recorded memory of the past. Having this experience made me realize the power that the subconscious mind has over us. Be very careful what you tell, show, or expose the subconscious mind to as it will record everything. It is like a non-judgmental recording device; it records everything and automates it for you. You do realize by now that you are doing things without really thinking. The subconscious mind makes these run effortlessly for you - walking, reaching, grasping, driving and so many other things. The subconscious mind is just a powerful instrument that but could also turn against you. Nowadays, many times, we are running on what I would call "automatic". Our beliefs, our Ego program, our reactions, reasons, and explanations are part of this. We are repeating the indoctrination that we were been feeding through our TV, repeat the explanations we were so easily given in debates, in the news, on social media more like that song playing in our mind comes up to us from time to time. We take it all in without realizing, through our subconscious mind, and they become part of our limitations programming, the Ego. It is easy to see why strong convictions are the standard of the day. Heated political and many times nasty debates, partisan opinions, what it looks like a continuous fight are running every day in the media. The standard of the day is a partisan media outlet spewing explanations and reasons on why the "other" side is bad, how they are good and even giving you many explanations why that is. It comes as no surprise that people experience the difficulty of identifying the truth and many decide that the truth is a relative term nowadays.

One of the most powerful sentiments is fear. The AI algorithms have proved it and the media outlets have already realized this and continue to induce automatic fear through their programs daily. It is no wonder so many human beings feel the negativity nowadays and refuse to watch and feed into it. My son is telling me to not watch the news because they are mostly negative, ugly, and sad. I was also telling my parents during my childhood that the TV tells us lies. We were not thinking about it much when we were kids, we just felt it and knew it. What is the younger generation or people around you tell you about the media nowadays?

Universal Consciousness

To my point, the subconscious mind takes it all in and memorizes it - images, sound, smells, feelings, emotions. It plays the recording when needed, takes over in cases of danger and defines part of our personality. It is very interesting to find out where that is all stored. Is it your mind or is it in a field that you can access and that somehow becomes part of the whole? Some say that we are all part of a common consciousness, proving it by showing that multiple scientific discoveries came about the same time in history in different locations of the world as well as world records were broken one after another as soon as someone broke one after many decades. Is this a way we communicate with each other? Is part of our subconscious mind being shared with the "field" and does it become part of the whole? Do we get part of the common knowledge via what we call intuition, gut feeling? Are these recordings of the subconscious becoming part of the divine wisdom and are these part of the Universe evolution? Are we in a playing simulation, a game made to continuously improve the Energy and Life? Thoughts, memories are all energy and as quantum physics demonstrated, the fact that the intention of the observer influences the experiment is interesting as well as fascinating. What you want is what you get. What you desire and expect should come. Do we create our own reality? Does the subconscious mind make this all happen through its interface with the universal consciousness? I do not have an answer for you, but I hope I gave you some insights and things to consider. I feel, though, that we are all One, we share a common consciousness, and the delimitation and impression of separation between each individual human beings are just an illusion created and sustained by our automatic limitations programing.

Ego Disturbances

Is this happening to you? You are good at a sport, an activity, but during that activity your thinking comes in the way. It could be triggered by you or by someone else. You might say in your mind – "Wow, how good I am at this!" Someone else might say - "You are doing great! You are so good at this!". Suddenly, you are just not doing so good anymore. Is it the observer being envious of your performance and in fact not rooting for you or is it your Ego limiting you? It could be both. Your Ego starts to awake, growing, feeling recognized - the Ego that many of us are identifying with. Being in the way, it is not able to help, it is just limiting you more by running its program. This clearly demonstrates to me that the Ego sometimes works in your disadvantage. If you would not engage the thinking and continue undisturbed, you will probably do as good at your game or better. Keep a serene, undisturbed, free your mind stance. Therefore, the best athletes are the ones with good self-control that are undisturbed by thoughts or comments like these. One of my friends says that the best you will be doing on an activity is at your second try, not the third, the fourth and so on. Is it maybe because the thinking goes in the way? The Ego disturbs the flow of energy, short-circuiting or affecting the initial intention. If we want to succeed, we need to have intention, faith or a strong will and a serene undisturbed mind that does not run all the possible failure scenarios continuously, taking all the good energy from the initial intention. In other words, to be without any doubts, to just believe in it.

Love is Coming to You and It is in You

Sometimes, we find out that a friend, someone close, has a challenge. There may be suffering involved. We do not know many times how to help. The person might even refuse help, or not even realizing that it needs help. Immediately after the event, I needed a lot of help. It was a 180% turn for me from almost never asking for help to needing help to even move, reach or eat. In these moments, I just learned to ask for help. In those moments, the Ego subsided, and I was able to do that. The Ego always stays in the way and remember, it is not helping, is just judging, and limiting us.

I was pleasantly surprised to feel the love, the empathy and the compassion of strangers, things I did not think that even existed anymore. From the women who advised me of the possible problem I was experiencing during the event and called the ambulance promptly, to the nurses and doctors taking care of me, people I never heard from in a long time or even human beings I never met, they all jumped to help. The Ego hides our inheriting good nature, and it is many times the one that dictates if we are in the "service to self" or "service to others" mentality.

Service

In these moments of needing help, you immediately feel who are your real friends and who are just using you or servicing themselves. I like to believe that the world is mostly populated by beings that are wanting to help others. It is easier to be of the "service to others" mentality and that is more rewarding and soothing. In the "Law of One" series, the channeled entity Ra is saying that you only need to be more than half (51%) of "service to others" to fit that category. We need the other 49% to take care of ourselves so we can serve others.

You see, it is never black and white as many times our Ego quickly judge. Everything is nuanced and balanced. You need to be 95% "service to self" to completely fit in that "service to self" category, though. To take this and now evaluate people based on these statements would be the wrong thing to do. "Service to others" and "Service to self" are just states of "mind" or more like states of consciousness. Even if you may immediately identify one or the other in someone, do not judge, we are all One, but we are all different. It is through these differences, the Creator experiences and learns it all.

Balancing

It happens to people that sometimes they get angry, a strong emotion manifesting inside them. This may be triggered by an event and amplified by memories and experiences of the past. This is happening when a great disturbance occurs inside and most of that energy concentrates on fear, the unhappiness created by something perceived as wrong or bad relative to self. It is the Ego that amplifies at that time and drives this. During that time, the person may also experience physical or mental pain, dizziness and so on. This is proving that letting the Ego roam free can wreak havoc through our body and soul. Many diseases start because of a body and/or soul imbalance.

In moments like these, it is important to remember that we are encompassing both good and bad, we are a part of all Creation. We should remember that at the core we are a serene balance of all that is happening with all Creation. In these moments, it is good to remember to balance the negative emotion with a positive one, which is also part of you, basically to balance it with the opposing emotion. This way, we balance ourselves out, we get closer to God, which is impartial. Remember the saying in the bible that all was going well until people started "to know the difference between good and bad"? At that time, we started judging, moving from good to bad and back, forming our own beliefs about what is good and what is bad and our Ego, our limitations programing, took hold of us. It would become clear now that choosing the middle path is the way to go and we can achieve this by sustaining a balance of feelings and emotions. This way, we are getting closer to God, and we are identifying better with Nature, the environment, and the Universe. Do not fight one side or the other, understand that you too are part of both.

The Good and Bad

The identification of good and bad and the fact that they present differently for different human beings got us to the polarization in media, the polarization between us and beyond.

Several churches and religious beliefs talk about heaven and hell, basically the good and bad. If you do good, you go to the heaven and if you do bad you go to the hell. I am interpreting this as in fact a state of your eternal soul. If your soul is tormented and full of remorse for things you may consider you did bad for others to maybe get yourself ahead of them by maybe being overbearing, that could be called hell. For heaven, that is the reward of an enlightened and happy soul, for the good it did and wished for others. It is basically like the difference between "service to self" and "service to others". You see situations in history when personalities, businesspersons and others are feeling remorse for the suffering they caused to others during their lifetime. They try to redeem themselves before their passing by leaving their accumulated riches to charities, trying to at least save the memory of their name for posterity by building public institutions or foundations serving the people. Look for these examples through all the American history, but especially during the Industrial Revolution.

So, choose wisely between an exalted or a tormented soul.

Reexperience

He did not experience the same exalted state for quite some time. He felt that he wanted to revisit that and go into that beautiful state again. It took a week of preparation of reading spiritual books and getting into himself, expressing the wish to help others, but also projecting the intention to reexperience that beautiful meditative state. This happened just at the end of the week when he started composing this book and his inspiration and creativity were at its highest levels in a long time. And it all happened again during the time when he was listening to an audio book, "The Feeling is the Secret" by Neville Goddard. He has realized later that the state lasted about 50 minutes. Those were all moments of pure joy. During the meditation, he was hearing the narration of the book, but it did not seem that he really paid attention to it or the intellect made any effort to understand it. Still, he felt he got the content, but it was like the words were going through him, rather than being analyzed by him. When he was experiencing that, he did not realize the time passing even if he was feeling alert and hearing things around him. He would not have the desire to move, but he was trying to do that to make sure he is there and can do it in this state. Yes, he was able to move, he tried hands and legs and was still able to experience the sensation of Joy. Eyes closed, he was lying on the bed, experiencing what cannot be described in words, but I will try to do it anyways.

At the beginning, he felt his body relaxing, relived of tension, especially felt the tension giving up in his hands and fingers. He then started seeing a blue light, deep blue, ultramarine, pulsating and coming from what it seemed like the back of his neck. At first, it appeared small and then grew wider but oscillating, becoming larger and smaller and being almost of a liquid consistency like blue ink on a black piece of plastic or paper, without a uniform shape. It was like liquid moving and shaping itself in different ways in what seemed like an irregularly curved mass, but on a single plane. There was no third dimension. The blue was growing and shrinking in a pulsating but not necessarily rhythmic pattern. It seemed like he was able to maintain the blue color spots and even growing them bigger by concentrating, to the point they will fill all the "visual" mind field. In the process, he was feeling that this was coming from the base of his head, like I mentioned, the back of his neck region. At times, in the pulsating movement, the blue "liquid" will fade and reappear brighter and wider and sometimes even filling the "canvas" completely. It will fade to a green a few times, sometimes will become an indigo to violet color, but it will still revert quickly to that beautiful blue. What it was amazing to him was that he was pretty much alert, his mind was able to even put questions during this, like - "Can I maintain this?", "What happens if I concentrate on the back of the neck region more?", "Let's try it!", "In what conditions will this stop and fade away?". He was seeing this not through his eyes, which were obviously closed, but through what it seems to be a region above, between his eyes, almost like in the mind. Was this the third eye? No way of telling, but what was for sure it was that he experienced this with so much joy and it was amazing to him that he was alert and able to sustain it. He would not want to get out of this state and wanted to stay there experiencing it and growing and shrinking the blue color veil at his will. It was one of the most beautiful experiences he had until then. At the end, he was getting out of the state as he clearly heard his son calling him to show him something. He responded, "Coming in two minutes" and even then, the game he was playing in his mind with the blue wave was still going. He heard his son coming into the room and saying - "Ahh, I will let you rest then". After that, he opened his eyes and got out of bed. At that point, the experience stopped. He felt a little nauseated after this, but that sensation quickly disappeared.

He was knowing now that something amazing was there inside his body, connected with his mind. He started to understand now what some of the limits are, where the mind comes into the equation and what is influencing what. The fact that he remained alert during the experience was still fascinating to him. He liked to think at that time, after this experience, that part of it was due to the opening of the creativity and communication energy center which is associated with the color blue. This was just the beginning and much more remained to be unveiled.

Balancing and Judging

Besides suppressing the judging ego, process which I call "gentling the ego", the balancing of the emotions and feelings is one of the keys to experience it all. Balancing the negative with positive is bringing you back in neutral where you have no bias, you do not fuel the ego so easily and you are closer to the Divine, which encompasses all good and bad. The opposite is true as well, even if you are not purposely balancing positive emotion with negative, oftentimes the subconscious is doing it for you in your sleep. After periods of bliss, you may experience bad dreams, nightmares, showing you that the "body" tries to balance these automatically. Listen to your body, notice but do not react by judging. The "body" performs this balancing act all the time. The judging that the ego performs is sometimes not only towards others, trying to justify why others are not right and you are, but to yourself. Do not judge yourself too harshly, be gentle with yourself and others, gentle your ego.

Modern Times

Are you reading the news daily or are you connecting through social media? I used to do the same until I experienced the freedom of not reading and not following. The mind, which is mainly a vehicle of storing and processing information is avid of getting more and more, getting into an obsession. Opening news sites to see what is new, watching or listening to the news in the background are some of these manifestations. One of my grandparents which was alone at the time was telling me that he must leave the radio on in the background to get rid of the loneliness. It is a common topic across elders. Many of them know more than anyone about what happens in the world today, what is the daily debate and so on. Now I realize that the TV and media in general changed lately and if you hang on to the debates and daily crazy you are sure to get into the rhythm that they intend, to keep you hooked to a continuous sentiment of fear, negativity and creating an addiction of wanting more of it. Your brain will then be surely looking for that continuous stimulation getting you further and further away from your inner happiness and into searching for external factors to create "happiness" for you. These factors are pushed through convenient advertising when the emotional factor of the program is at its peak. We are then sure to become a collection of thoughts, needs and "addictions" that drive our life. The freedom of not needing, not knowing the latest news, not following the latest trends is refreshing. You will ask yourself why that is going on, why is this not stopping since many are seeing it as bad for them?

Well, as we have a reason to say this is bad, they have a reason to say this is good. There are two facets of the story. We cannot change the world through reasoning because everyone has their own reasoning. Since Adam and Eve realized what is good and bad, the issue perpetuated.

Reasoning

Every human being decides what is good and bad through reasoning. The issue is that this reasoning is going on in our minds and each one of us, besides some common social norms and common beliefs have our own reasoning. Due to this, if we want to resolve what we consider important world problems, things that have not been resolved for centuries, we in fact need to get rid of the reasoning. Some will say, get rid of the Ego. I say that this is partially true, but the Ego is just the bias part of it. One of my friends mentioned the fact that will not be good to put reasoning aside since that way we will lose the authenticity of the individual. I would say - "indeed only in a way" because we are in fact living in an illusion of separation and false individuality. We are all interrelated and we are One. If now you feel a space, a "hole" in your mind, a lack of words an absence of "thinking" or "reasoning" about this idea, it is probably because our mind cannot give us a solution, cannot reason about this or "think" about this because the mind has created this illusion itself. Seems that by limiting the reasoning we can achieve the Oneness and achieve that divine agreement which is in all of us. So, for what I can get from here, getting rid of the reasoning brings us to the One we all are. Being able to manifest our Oneness, we can resolve what we call the "world's problems" and get to the meaning of life.

Enlightenment and Existential Questions

Does this happen to you? You are driving your car and you feel that the Divine is with you, experiencing all you see, feel, and do. You also feel that the Divine is driving you, guides you. This is just a metaphor, because you know you are physically driving, but you feel the Divine driving you from a spiritual perspective. The key is to continue to listen, to open up, clear your blockages and opposing energies. These energies are many times driven by our mind – both sides, the conscious and unconscious, and also by what is called "karma" which would be for me the memory of the body and soul. Many times, you have what you consider bad memories in your mind, your heart (emotions), your body, your soul. Your ancestry memories live through your body template and pattern, physically in the memory of your cells. These all may be staying in the way of your enlightenment. You may call this bad "karma" and that can be any attachment that you consider bad or limiting - a thought, a memory, a place, an experience, a trauma or even something you may not know it happened with your ancestors or in a previous life. The necessity of "burning" of the bad karma, the reconciliations of these is essential for achieving that lasting awakened state and being able to open your energy centers so the divine energy flows freely through you. This I say is how you become connected, enlightened. It is many times a gradual process, but it can also happen suddenly after or during a traumatic event. You feel in these moments the love around you. You start realizing that you have a higher connection and somehow you may feel that time does not matters or does not exist anymore. To be able to stay there, it requires what I would call "discipline", like self-control, mindfulness and to continue to practice and growing on the spiritual path. Read, practice, evolve, meditate, walk in nature under the energy of the sun, clear your mind, gentle your ego, burn your karma, love yourself and others, love the nature and creation around you, connect with the energies of the Universe, stop, and ask yourself questions that appear to have no answers:

Who am I?
Why I am here?
What is my purpose in life?
What is the reason of all creation?
What is the Universe?
Why is the Universe infinite?
Are there multiple Universes?
Why do planets and stars exist and how were they created?
Do aliens exist?

and so on ...

The seeker will eventually get answers to at least some of these, answers that may not have meanings outside Self and answers that may not even be explained in words, but these will likely be beautiful answers.

Manipulation and Pitfalls

Many authors with best of intentions produce writings that may sound like a campaign of evangelization. Many times, spiritual writings sound rough to us because the intention of infringing to our free will is obvious. This may have worked in the past but during current times, it is immediately recognized. That is one of the pitfalls for us as well, as we grow through the spiritual path. We may feel that at one point by going through so many books, teachings, and experiences, we have the answer which then we may try to impose on others, to evangelize it. I think this is the wrong thing to do because each of us have our own path, we resonate to different things, and we believe in different things. We may look like we believe in the same, but we in fact each have our nuanced interpretation of the same. So, when you read this writing do not take it as trying to give a recipe to this or that, not even as a guide as it is just an experience, and it is what resonates with me. Take from it only what resonates with you, if anything, and do not look back.

Mainstreaming Template

Many of us are caught in what I call the template of mainstreaming, a template created by the society and a result of standardized learning and popular culture. Because we are all going through this process, the Universe of people is less divers, and the world is full of look-alikes. Mainstreaming and look-alikes are a crowded field. God wants to experience it all, the unrestricted, through you not through the templates that we put around us and reality. That is why getting out of mainstreaming, manifesting your un-limited creativity, and having an unfiltered experience is part of finding the Divine within you.

Continuing The Path

He was able to manifest things easier. With now less audio stimulation, he will drift into the trance in which the blue pulsating light still appeared. He will still hear the things going on around him and will not want to go out of that beautiful state in which the pulsating blue light was keeping him. The moments were not lasting more than one hour, but it was enough to lighten his day and evolve him slowly to a higher vibration and dimension. This beautiful meditative state was still relatively hard to achieve as the lower density three-dimensional world was dragging and easily distracting him. But he was now sure that he was on the right track since it became easier to him to achieve this meditative state.

Commercialization of The State of Mind

There are teachers which are fast to show you the right way to meditate and to evolve spiritually. From retreats to programs and books, to online videos preached by New Age prophets, there are so many. It is my opinion that there is no right way, a standard and a sure way to evolve spiritually. Each of us has our own way. What you listen to and watch, read and are taught can only be the catalysts as there is no template that works for everyone. Everyone can experience the Divine and each experience it in their own ways. There are no recipes. Like in life, some things work for some, other ones, work for others. So, do not be discouraged if you cannot go into meditation by doing specific things like repeating mantras or listening to music, poems, readings, like your friend is saying they are doing. There is no standard way. Each of us resonates to different things based on our background and particularities. Stay out of the commercialization of the state of mind and choose your own way.

The Higher Self

From what I gather from these experiences, it is that raising your frequency is the way you get to communicate with your essence, the way to connect to another invisible dimension of you and this can be achieved through meditation, through quieting of your logical mind.

Does this happen to you? Going outside in nature, you realize that you have a higher self that is always with you. This higher and pure You is watching over you from a different dimension. Your body is the vehicle that experiences the three-dimensional world now and that helps your higher self to evolve. Your higher self learns from your three-dimensional experience, even though your higher self is so wise. Learn to listen to your higher self by evolving spiritually. You are much more than your body and mind, you are your higher self too and that is where you are connected to the Divine, to the Life Energy. There are many more things to learn, to experience, realize and manifest and I will be happy to share my interpretation. And once again, please do not take everything literally, remember that there is no template, there is no absolute of anything and all of us are different but united. If these beliefs, thoughts, observations, and remarks do not resonate to you, do not give it a second thought, and forget about them. Feel the love of your family and friends, send your love to your fellow being and travel the Universe, my fellow seeker.

Modern Times and Suffering

For the modern beings, the suffering is oftentimes self-inflicted, automatic, and assumed. Have you ever been to grocery shopping in the weekend, to one of the big shops which claim to have everything under the sun for you? The scene is one like the bumper cars at the fair. A large mass of people in a relatively restless and dissatisfied state of mind "running" to get what they decided they need, many times not finding what they were looking for and wandering from isle to isle, oftentimes ending buying much more than they came for. The scene continues with the search of their car in the immense parking lot, the loading, the drive itself, the unloading and sorting through items to decide what goes where. This is another way of "suffering" created by the modern society. By the time all is done, you are sure to be tired, be exposed to lots of false advertising and lost 2-3 hours which you could have used going outside and spending quality time with your family and friends. Skip the big shop, simplify your life by going to more pleasant and more outdoor experiences like the local farmer's market, go to smaller, less busy, and healthier shops, buy less, and limit the pollution and waste.

The same type of situation happens when many crowd the roads and airports during national holidays or busy vacation seasons, trying to reach the intended destination, which most everyone is going to. Many times, the outings or the vacations during these times result in more stress and people feeling more tired after coming back. There are always things going on, the everyday struggle to survive and provide, the fact that there is always something to do at work and at home. These are all sure to get us away from experiencing the energy of life, from the love around us, distancing us from knowing our divine self. Many decide they do not have time to go outside or to meditate. They cannot get out of this induced state, always "needing something", always on the hunt for something, always competing on something with someone, always on the run, always busying the mind with what and who did that or the other. It is played that way that it basically becomes an addiction, something that several indigenous nations described as the madness of the people coming to visit and colonize them. Madness is how they characterized this never-ending search for something material, something to fulfill them. This "madness" manifests in extreme cases through greed and can lead to tragic consequences. The modern society triggers changes in the way people think and act and we need to be aware of that, to manifest great self-control and take care and protect ourselves. The actors of the modern age look for "victims" to control, influence, and maneuver. Stay true to your core self, remember that none of this technology and economic pressure defines you at your core. Try to make it all better for your mind, body, and soul. This will also make it better for the ones around you which will see and start understanding your ways. Even if they may not agree with your ways, they will notice and may start thinking about it. But make no mistake, do not try to convince, and influence others as each of us has their own free will.

Frequencies of Earth and Mind

There has been a lot of talk about the Earth frequencies, about the fact that they are changing and moving Earth and the human beings that are ready to "graduate" to another density. I must admit that it is a beautiful and fascinating concept which we cannot be sure is true. In any case, my understanding is that this has to do with the Earth frequencies as well. The 7.83hz which is the primary resonance frequency of Earth, even though it varies slightly, it influences our life. Our theta and alpha brain waves are close to this frequency of Earth, and they are matching with that when we are at rest. The brain waves are changing their frequency based on what we are doing, what our state of mind is. For this, being connected, achieving the meditative state, getting us synched to the base Earth resonance frequency is the illuminate state, the one that gets us in communication with the energies of the Universe. We have more theta brain waves as kids until we start speaking and start occupying our minds with reasoning, problems to solve and worries. Getting us in sync with the frequencies of the Earth may connect us to the Divine and implicitly create a better world where we love and understand each other, a world where the personal ambitions, the self-created Ego is suppressed, and we all are in service to each other.

Dreams and Previous Lives

Is this happening to you? Sometimes you have nightmares. Out of nowhere, a bad horrible dream is impressing upon you. It happens that you feel this most heavy feeling and it is like you know that an imaginary situation is triggering it. The cause of the feeling may have shown to you before in another dream. As we grow our awareness, we pay more attention to feelings, to what is happening around us, to what our subconscious mind is "saying". Does this happen to you? - waking up during the night and thinking that that was due to a nightmare, even though you may just wake up due to the physiological need to go to the bathroom. These waking up moments in the middle of a dream make us realize and remember the dream. We are influenced by so many factors, some of us may be affected by lives that we lived before. We may remember these in our dreams. These inexplicable nightmares with apparently no relation to us and somehow seen from the perspective of an outside observer may be an awful event that in fact marked us profoundly in a previous incarnation or even something that is happening now around us, our neighborhood or our city, something that we are very sensible to. There is no way of telling but we should realize that the bad dreams might be consuming and due to this, sometimes we may wake up tired in the morning and not realizing why. Is this what hell is referring to? The continuous tormenting of the soul we sometimes feel in the nightmares.

It is up to us to clean and purify our soul and enrich it with goodness.

The Void

As I was experiencing the blue colored fractals more and more in deep meditation, I also realized how hard it is for us to attain that state and go beyond. The mind seemed to have a perversity of its own, trying to intervene in the experience and interrupt it. It enters a repeating cycle that is being filled with thoughts and justification coming from the fear of experimenting something different than we should. If the mind sees something that you perceive from your education as abnormal or impossible, it immediately enters in a filling and fear mode, ultimately filling that with something else that is more familiar or known. But just this unknowing, this complete giving up and experiencing the "void" is the key for us to connect with who we really are. Do not be afraid of the space, the void in your thoughts.

Angel Reiki Sessions

I did not believe in Reiki. I knew, though, that energetical healing and balancing is real. I participated to Reiki classes but grew to consider Reiki a very subjective matter and reserved to gifted practicians. As I was debating that in my mind trying to find justifications of why this does not work and why this is just the trend of the moment, a dear family friend was reaching out and offering to do Angel Reiki sessions on me to improve my wellbeing and alleviate the pain and aches that my recovery was putting me through. The synchronicity was amazing, especially since I did not communicate with the friend for several months. I never expressed the interest in Reiki to her and never told her I am going through a Reiki class just out of curiosity, to see how it can help. What followed was amazing and during one of these sessions, this project you are reading now, and its name were suggested to me in meditation.

From the first session I felt my hands warming up, radiating, and the part of my body that I touched felt pulsating in sync with the glow in my hands. A warm pleasant pulsating sensation filled my body. From the second session, I was starting to see blue fractals like in the deep meditation, supplemented for brief moments by sparkles. It was amazing and I was looking forward to seeing where this can get. I learned again to not judge, to not reject something my mind cannot understand and to be open to anything.

On the third session, even before it started, I had a sensation of my arms and legs getting softer and I was able to temporarily do some movements that I was not able to do after the event. This state started before the session and lasted maybe 30 minutes after. During the session, I was beginning to feel a pulsating rhythm and energy flowing through the region between the eyebrows and felt it residually for some time afterwards as well. Besides the blue "light" patterns that were coming and going, pulsating, and continuously reshaping and at times flowing to a purple nuance, I experienced colors changing to mustard green for brief moments when I ultimately felt a complete stillness, what it seemed like the eternal, nothing moving, nothing changing, no time passing state. It was the Ultimate, it was something special. These stillness moments will flicker back to the blue fluid fractal light and for very brief moments will come back again. All in all, I could say I experienced 3 or 4 of these eternal moments in a 30-minute session.

These moments of stillness increased in number and duration on the next sessions and something new appeared. They were some types of blurry images, nothing I could make sense particularly of. They looked like nice bright landscapes seen through a magnifying glass, like you see the background in a portrait picture.

The green aura stillness moments as well as the blue energy visualization would be common occurrences on the following sessions. Additionally, I experienced some new phenomenon which looked like an energy transmission. This felt like a sudden vibration burst, similar to what you would feel when you start a car, but deeper inside.

At the end of these sessions, I would feel somewhat lightheaded and that especially was the sensation on the first ones. That sensation will fade rather quickly after the session. After each of these meditative states, I would see the world differently, with more understanding, compassionately and from the perspective of what is seemed to be the universal Love.

During one of the sessions, my mind was wandering and started imagining different things. One was Jesus that took my hand, and we were floating effortlessly above. At one point, I was touching his golden hair with my hand, and I was wowed and wondering. Then I am not sure if him suggested it, or I just had a sensation that my guides are with me.

Somehow, I also received the understanding that at least two of them are my maternal grandmother and my paternal grandfather. A moment of ultimate stillness came at the time when the archangel Michael came to mind. In this imagined thing, it was suggested that my son and the daughter of a family we are friends with came here as incarnated souls to help our souls, my wife's, and mine.

I will continue to experience the ultimate stillness moments on the next sessions. Even though, sometimes it was hard to enter in the meditative state, it was possible for me to enter the state after no more than 10 of 15 minutes of relaxation in bed. I would fall asleep sometimes, even though this was not common. I would, at times, "hear" the word God repeated multiple times in what seemed like wow moments, one after another. This felt good and filled my heart with love, which I will then start spreading and sending in form of red hearts to each of the family members, friends, and relatives I would visualize separately. I felt then how my face was shaping itself to show the most natural smile, the smile of love. And it will stay like this for minutes on end like it will be inscribed in eternity. Is this what the Buddhists call "smile-down". It was amazing to me how this smile will stay effortless on my face, like the muscles were relaxing into it. It was the joy, the beauty, the pleasure, the eternal light. At the same time, I would feel something like an energy, or current entering my head from above, right above the forehead, from somewhere above the eyes. This "current", more like a flow, seemed to feed the meditative state and to sustain it. Even if I would hear everything around me, no other rebel thoughts would enter my mind. Is this the feeling when you are one with the flow of the Universe? Is this a snapshot of Nirvana? After about maybe 20 minutes like these, which seemed like an eternity, this brought me to a state where out of the sudden I would start hearing a loud vibration, more like a buzz, or ringing in both ears, which will modulate in time to a louder and higher frequency getting to a very loud high pitch noise. This got me a little scared. I was in that "ringing ears" phase for maybe 30 seconds when the mind interfered "saying" that I need to get out of that state, which I did, and the ringing suddenly disappeared, getting me back to the regular daily stream of thought as I got out of bed. I was back to the egotistic condition of our daily lives. It would have been interesting to continue to see what would have happened next with the ringing vibration, but it looks like fear interfered. This proves that we are afraid to have different spiritual experiences and to hear and see things we were thought that we are not supposed to. The habits and education that we went through for so many years interferes and says "NO", like pushing a big red button. Let's see what the next experience will bring and if the "SAFETY" mechanism can be overridden.

The Living Food

But what about food? Listening to several gurus I got to learn why eating healthy and ethically is important. There are even scientifical experiments that shown that just your thought of eating a specific thing, let's say an egg, triggers a response in that egg like that egg would become excited that it will become part of something bigger as you, the human being and beyond. I also learned that eating every day something fresh, like fruits or raw vegetables containing cells that are still alive is important. That energy of life transfers to you and energizes you. Eating is not only about chemistry, the minerals, vitamins, lipids, proteins, sugars you take in but also about the energy of life.

We hear many times that water is very important for you. Indeed, especially nowadays when we eat a lot of dry foods, there is an extra need for hydration. Still, an excess of water intake can be poison for our body. What the spiritual gurus teach us by paying attention to their bodies is to "eat the water, not drink the water". In other words, they teach us to eat softer foods, containing more water, like fruits, vegetables, soups, etc. That is the ideal way to balance our bodies.

The Energy of Life

Then what about the energy of life? Did you know that each life form is animated by the energy of life and this energy shows and is represented by the blue color. Learning about this energy present everywhere, after experiencing the blue color visualizations during deep meditation, made me think that what I am "seeing" there may in fact be the energy of life. In these moments after a deep meditation, I will put my hand over my third eye, and with my eyes still closed "I will see" millions of whitish-yellow dots that look like static. Are the "blue" colors and the whitish-yellow dots visualizations of the energy generated by me or is this energy all around me and I am just tuning to the environment? Is this blue fluid image that I am visualizing, in fact, my energy? I have no way of saying just yet, but I am interested to complete some experiments and see the tangible proofs of this energy in action. I will include more details about it further down the line as I seek more about these.

Learning to Notice

Is this happening to you? You go outdoors in nature, relax, feel at peace, and you are amazed that you now see and notice things that you never noticed before - from the simplest things like leaves and seeds falling, to more intricate things. Try the following. Away from the sun, look at the blue sky on a beautiful sunny day. Try to first concentrate looking at an imaginary point close to you. For sure do not look towards the sun and try to stay in the shade. It may take a while but try not to think about anything. If you spend enough time, you may see a multitude of very fine luminescent particles "dancing", doing what seem like pulsatory, randomly changing moves. Then try to further relax your eyes, remove the close focus, and try to see the big picture. Same "dancing" particles show across the background of the blue sky. They are also easily visible across a white background, like the house fascia or the siding. Is this real? What is this? Why did I not notice this before? As soon as something more important comes in the mind to think about, you do not pay attention to them and basically do not notice them anymore. Can these be energy particles stimulating life? Is this the energy of life? Tao? God? All these are very good questions, but this is proof that we are oftentimes only noticing what we expect to see and what we are looking for. All the other aspects remain unnoticed if they do not match our knowledge, education, and experience template. Let's really look, watch, and notice. Ultimately, this was the main purpose of the mind in the first place, to observe and notice, not to judge and analyze. We only notice if we are really looking.

Soul Evolution

So, what are we? Are we a collection of likes and dislikes? Are we what we enjoy? I would say that we are exactly what we choose and want to be. The free will is very powerful and meant for us to allow to experience everything. It is more about soul evolution, this ultimate experience where we get to see all aspects of life with good and bad. But as we realized by now, what we might consider a bad experience is nothing else but an experience which might bring us to the Ultimate. Strong, bad feelings and emotions that we learn how to conquer, notice, and understand get us closer to understanding our journey to nothingness.

Oftentimes, we try to fit in, to cling to the latest billionaire fad of the day and in fact succumb to the mainstream. Still, in doing that we give away our identity, we limit our experience, we become slaves of the mainstream and commerce. Our identity and uniqueness are expressed through our heritage, our cultural and spiritual experience of the current and prior lives. We get pushed by the continuous bombardment of news, advertising, and fads to abandon our heritage and experience and replace it with what I call mainstreaming. This is the thing you hear being referred as "brain washing", term which is recently ridiculed, but which in fact is very actual and important. What will we be without our heritage and our experience? What will we be just by following a "mainstreamed" and standardized experience dictated by the billionaires of the moment as a profitable and meaningful experience? God, the Universe want us to experience it all and to become one with Self and share the experience with the whole.

And there you go, let go, let the soul experience the life fully, one that is not driven by the mainstream and dogma.

Instead of clinging to the latest fad and listening to other mainstreamers promoting their empty message, we could make the world better by communicating and learning from others, holding space for someone close, expressing our love and being close to a human being. So many people are feeling alone and are not being listened to, being also pushed by the societal norms to keep it quiet and suffer inside. Everyone has a right to be heard, not only the billionaires of the moment. So, be free, experience it all, communicate and do not forget to also have fun, celebrate, laugh to the fullest. There is plenty to enjoy around. I have a simple measure to all this. If something is bringing you joy and you find yourself smiling to it, it is probably good for you. Experience and enjoy!

Loneliness

Many people are feeling alone. Especially when the quiet settles, many of us do not know what to do. A sense of emptiness coupled with some flavor of sadness and sorrow towards self-settles in. As I was giving the example of some of the grandparents and parents filling this empty space with radio and TV programs, many are in fact so afraid of being "alone". But we are never alone. It is us that are always monitored by the higher self, we are never alone in a pure sense.

Especially when the Holidays period approaches, the reality settles in. That is when many are realizing the shell of multiple so-called friendships and the so-called relatives that just do not find the time to call, send a message or acknowledge you. The people that do not come through in these moments are hurting the ego. The ego usually responds with either repulsion, disappointment or even tries to amplify itself by trying to broad its influence. And so, it comes that some use their money to buy expensive presents or vacations to attract – to be read "steal" - the friends and family members on their side, a way to in fact reward their ego in hopes of recognition and the absolute need to not be forgotten. This is just an unsubstantial shell, though.

The Holidays could indeed be a period of strong, contradictory feelings. Besides recognizing the shell of many false friendships, this period could become a voyage to self-discovery, a time of awakening, a time where we turn the page and recognize our interior beauty and the love we feel inside. Instead of self-judging or judging the persons that do not come through, we should recognize the love emanating from our hearts and in fact be compassionate for people that do not feel it and are always on the lookout for external validation and interaction.

The same happens with some parents wanting their children to visit for the Holidays and when they arrive, they just talk to them about trivial things or watch TV, not really connecting with them. Their ego wants this recognition of feeling important and recognized, to not be forgotten, but when it in fact is getting that, it completely forgets about the others. You can see a similar interaction in the social media and messaging apps. To "squeeze" a Happy Holidays! you are realizing with some that you must be the initiator of the conversation. When you get a reciprocated "automated" response like that, you can identify when it comes as a egotistic response since in fact the recipient does not even recognize your statement in their response but just tries to amplify their ego status by emphasizing their "more important" message. Your words, your wishes remain unacknowledged, and the person continues on with their message. The communication almost becomes a monologue. So to say, your words fall on deaf years. Oftentimes, the unbalanced energies generated by unprocessed emotions of different persons you interact with are being expressed in these messages.

You may be on the receiving end of these unprocessed emotions or feelings. Do not let these affect you, but also do not reject them on the receiving end and realize with compassion that these may be an expression of misfortunes or mistreatment the person experienced before. You cannot help by giving a resolution here, as these feelings can only be processed by the person voicing them. All we can do is to provide understanding, compassion, and a space for the person to express and have time to initiate the processing of these feelings.

And so, you can realize how automated, impersonal, fake, and at the same time complex and misleading the interaction can be. Interactions that seem awkward are many times that expression of frustrations or unprocessed feelings and emotions.

Always look for genuine interaction, genuine people and be recognizant of love versus ego amplification and driven interest. It is better to spend ten minutes of genuine interaction with genuine and loving people than hours of empty interaction with interest driven people. Provide a space of recognition, quiet and attentive listening, understanding and compassion for those that are not doing that. Do the same for self. Recognize the love inside, your higher self, choose wisely, help others, and live to the fullest and you will never be alone.

Not Caring for Either

Can the society be explained through the lenses of the soul evolution process? I think it can.

You may remember from the history lessons about the periods of unending wars and conflict.

It was a time when many souls wanted to experience these things, for them to evolve to the next level. It was in fact a collective shift that happened with these.

So, you may have seen information in several books and articles about turning circles and shifts documented on specific years. I would say that these may tangibly touch on the concept, but the evolution cannot possibly be linked to an empiric timeline like 100 years cycles or specific year shifts. The shifts happen when a critical mass of souls have learned what they desired to learn and incline the balance towards something new. We only really "see", notice, the level of evolution that we are on. We peripherally see the other souls on other levels, but either we do not give them much attention, are uninteresting to us, or even worst, we are outraged by their actions.

This happens in day-to-day interaction as well when being aware and mindful of your surroundings and realizing that you are on another frequency with the being you may try to interact with. You may say that you became "invisible" for these beings, and they become "invisible" to you. Suddenly, for the mindful, awakened person you realize that what you categorized as annoying noise before, clears out and makes space for the real path, the middle path, your path. Could this be the middle path that Buddhists and Taoists are talking about? I think it is. A path that, as one of my friends observed, is defined by "not caring for either". The observation is valid as you will not be clinging to the extremes, and you are not being influenced by the distractions or obstacles on the sides. Actively being able to clear these distractions, to remove "the noise" on the periphery, is essential to our soul evolution.

Soul Business

But what about business? A business can be a primal way for a young soul to experience material things and gouge large sums of money, but for an older soul, a business is really about impacting people's life and supporting them in their soul evolution. Therefore, I say the future of a business is to become a "soul business". You may have noticed that advertising becomes more intrusive, more expensive, but at the same time less efficient. It becomes that annoying factor we do not care for, the thing that we dread during a favorite show, video, podcast, movie, or game. It is that way because less and less of us are interested in these and the fact that we recognize the unethical message in many of them. We are less and less interested because advertising is mostly effective when presented to young souls. More evolved souls are more aware, more mindful and do not cling to these material sales messages anymore. Exactly as in a prior example, we start to filter this noise and get on our middle path. The future is of the businesses that recognize the soul evolutions, evolve with them, facilitate these evolutions and are even compassionate in a way by not trying to egotistically conquer all the market as we have seen in the past when many monopolies appeared.

Taking Care of Your Body

As you become more aware of your surroundings and pay more attention to your body, you recognize what its needs are, and you notice the signals that it gives you. It will "tell" you when it needs to move, when it needs to eat, when it needs to relax. Taking care of your body is key to achieve more awareness, to be able to have longer meditative states, to gain the time to reflect and be able to discover the mysteries of life. Take care of your body, so you can be rich in spirit.

Many times, if we do not have the mindfulness and the awareness, we do not even realize the addictive effects of things like sugary foods.

Does this happen to you? You put a plate of delicious sweets on a plate on a table or counter. Every time you pass nearby, your mind is telling you – "I would like myself one of these. They are so good..." and you may even salivate, and your stomach may growl. In no time, you realize that all the sweets are disappearing, like all the members of your household would be in an eating competition. If you have the awareness, you may realize in those moments what power the subconscious mind has over you by craving for these quick rewards of energy boosts, like eating sugar. We should see if this principle applies to other situations. I think it does. There is a shaming expression that goes around these days – "instant gratification". It is just the same thing. Our brain becomes "addicted" to these quick rewards, like the energy boost from the sweets as well as other processes that provide reward, pleasure, satisfaction.

Being aware of these is essential in our evolution.

But how can we be aware of these to take care of our body in a good way? We all know that sugar in excess leads to obesity as well as many illnesses.

Knowing how to avoid the "addictive" situations means taking care of our body in a good way. Avoiding situations that lead to energetical imbalances is something we should pay attention to. I realized that every time an energetical imbalance comes into play, being caused by either a situation, nutrition, over exertion, etc., it leads to unwanted repercussions - an unwell state of the body and mind which stalls or slows down the spiritual progress.

Physical activity as well as fresh air and sun exposure are also essential to our well-being. Exactly as in the hospital when I was craving sun and fresh air, I was also craving body movement. Our body is made to move, it needs to stretch and be active to feel good and function optimally. Not moving enough can lead to muscle weakness, constipation, tiredness, and many other issues. Because the inactivity limits the interaction and the experience, it can even lead to mental issues. Immediately after being starting the OT and PT, I experienced what I would call the "joy of movement", that feeling of joy and happiness our body experiences when it moves and participates in the environment. Many of us take this for granted, not realizing that it is an important part of our happiness. Experiencing and moving in different environments, as well as interacting with it and other beings gives us that ultimate joy, we take for granted, joy which we may not even notice and appreciate until we lose it. So, listen to your body, go out, experience, move, exercise, and enjoy.

On Top of The World

After the event, as he started feeling better, his wife brought him the computer and tablet at his request. He was feeling the need to occupy the mind with something. The tablet experience brought him more of a passive experience with videos and shows on Netflix of sorts. It was enjoyable but nothing out of the ordinary. It has been weeks after the event since he got a hold of his computer, and when he "reunited" with it, it was a very interesting experience. For some reason, he was feeling on top of the world when using it. He was feeling like he would remotely control the world. This was something he have never noticed before as a software engineer and young executive.

Analyzing and processing my feelings I had during that time, I realized that this is probably what the computer coupled with the Internet does to us. It is an amplification of self. The fact that it was my computer with all my personal files and access like links and accounts stored on it, made me feel important. The fact that at a click of touchpad I was going to see that, check that and command different services to do this and that, like ordering or scheduling things, seemed magical. I realized that this gets us in a way addicted to our devices, especially the computers, which allow us to amplify our presence, to express our creativity and share it with others. Using them, we become a master controlling the world. Our self-perceived importance increases.

Fatalism or Not?

As you may hear or read discourses on religious and societal topics, you may realize that oftentimes these are pushing things towards some kind of fatalistic approach. It is being said that this and that is the right path, and you should conform to so and so, that such so will be a good path for you, for everyone and what is written will happen, what is supposed to happen will happen, what the norms say you need to follow, that so and so is the right path to follow to the "light...". Just that in fact all is mostly a trial-and-error situation, a learning experience. This way it is in life, it is in business, it is in relationships. What will life be if we will only follow a set of norms, rules and already drawn paths? Yet, the society and the religion are expecting us to do so. Life is to be experienced, though, as is and be as authentic as can be and not to be seen through a fatalistic approach.

Reality Creation

There has been talks about creating our own reality and experiencing your own vision.

Just take a minute and picture the perfect life for you. Imagine the perfect health, the perfect job or business, what you consider and rate as the best food, enjoy the perfect entertainment, the perfect relationship and something that the words cannot express, and it seems perfect to you. Many times, we limit our imagination to something that can be described in words. But make no mistake, what can be described in words is oftentimes filtered by our ego. Much more beautiful is what cannot be described in words and ego in fact cannot filter. Sit comfortably, imagine this perfect you, perfectly interacting with the environment and others. Feel the love that surrounds you - the happiness, the joy of the moment. "Ahhh...". The whole world loves you, the environment is perfect, you are perfect, you are the creating force of the Universe. You create your own reality and transform the reality for others; transform the way they see everything.

Have fun, have a big laugh, enjoy yourself. You are on top of the world!

How is this phrase sounding in your head now? - "Nothing is perfect!". Does it have any meaning anymore? It is all relative, it is the way you see it - "Everything is perfect". Let it be. You are the creator.

Feelings

As you become more aware about your ego, your self-talk and sense the feelings and emotions generated inside you, you start to differentiate between what is real or not. Feelings of sadness, betrayal, anger, frustration can all be very powerful and take hours on end to process. They can generate a very powerful energetical imbalance that can linger for a long time, may cause disease and can be for sure very consuming. As soon as they take hold of your energy, it is very hard to stop them as they are self-fueling. It is incredible, but the ego thrives on this energy as well continuing to re-fuel these feelings with it. You are like in a centrifuge, pushed to the sides when all this energy wreaks havoc in the middle of your soul and body. As soon as it takes off, it is very hard to stop. That is why it is important to recognize the early signs of these imbalances and remove the fuel and the actions of the ego that amplifies them.

You can always pinpoint feelings. They are the states you can identify consciously. But what about emotions, the feelings you experience subconsciously, and you do not know where they are coming from?

As we know emotions manifest first, many times triggered by a subconscious factor. Emotions might develop into feelings when we "process" these emotions through our thinking. Feelings might develop into moods.

As we become more self-aware, we can easily identify our emotions, feelings, reactions, and moods and make sense of them. Learn and take time to notice, listen and understand your natural response.

Music

Why is music creating us feelings? When I was a child, I was listening to a lot of music. Any kind of it and more. I would match the music with my feelings at the time or with the feelings I wanted to experience. I would be down, and I would want to feel happy or powerful and so on. I would crank a different kind of music for each of this. It would be harder then as we only had cassettes, tapes, CDs, or records. All of this changed in the last couple decades with the unlimited streaming where you can pop the music you want, any time you want. No wonder the huge popularity of it. Is music streaming one of these soul businesses? Maybe it is.

But what is about music? I feel the ultimate pleasure when listening to music that "vibrates" with my inner being, my soul. Sometimes I pay attention to the lyrics, but most of the times they are not important to me. Pay attention to the type of music that makes your heart exalted. Is there a direct connection between music, your soul, and your subconscious?

The relation with the subconscious is supported by the fact that these rhythms repeat in your mind at unexpected times, like I was mentioning, sometimes when waking up in the morning.

There are virtually no two human beings that like absolutely the same music.

Music also reminds us of specific moments in our life, moments and experiences connected to feelings. It also reminds us of our "identity", our cultural heritage and that we are in fact unique. The Ego thrives in that and rejoices that, but at the same time the soul realizes that this makes the global consciousness richer. So, the music satisfies both the ego as individuality and the soul as aspiring to become One. That is why music is so powerful. Give it some thought. What do you think?

Is this the key to open the way? Satisfying both the ego and the soul or more like keep the ego occupied and happy as you then bypass it and go beyond it. You may just be realizing now that the ego and the soul are not exclusive and do not oppose each other. So, listen to more music!

Can we influence our feelings and mood through music? I would say yes. Try it and feel what listening to different music opens in you.

Taking Care of Others and Self

Did you sometimes see yourself in a struggle to balance how much you care for others and how much time and resources to allocate to yourself? You probably feel most of the time that people are just looking out for themselves. Even if that may not be absolutely true, it may seem to you that way and strike you because you may be different and, in contrast, maybe more considerate and doing much for others. You might see that others do not share the same convictions and might not respond the way you expect. You may be immersed in the experience and enjoy the reward of helping others and completely forget about yourself. It is interesting to note that the ego gets preoccupied with both situations. You may be finding yourself bragging about self for doing much for others but also judging yourself for doing too much and not allowing enough time and resources for self. So, what it looks like a good thing at the beginning can lead at the end to suffering and an internal fight between these forces which the ego fuels on.

It is important to realize, though, that we will really be happy only when we strike a balance and quiet this internal struggle. You should always remember that you have a choice, the choice is always yours. You should indeed be sensitive to the experience and suffering of others and help but that should also not outweigh the importance of You. If you are always inclined to help others in detriment of self, always think that you are also a human needing the same. Show yourself the same gratitude, compassion, and respect. Remember to love yourself the same as you love others. This should break the circle of convulsive patterning our ego might go in sometimes as you are stuck between dilemmas.

The reverse is also true. If you find valuing yourself more than valuing others, remember that in essence we are all One, even if we are behaving and looking differently. Love others as equally as you love yourself.
As you get in balance, there will not be much for the ego to say anymore. It will be quiet. The inner voice will not find any more threats to "complain" about and it will feel "safe" because - "What is the ego, in fact?" It is just a guardian there for us to keep our physical existence safe. There is nothing to blame the ego about. If anything, the ego should be itself understood. Be compassionate with your ego and it will be your best friend.

The Game of Life

Being of software engineering background, going through my experiences, and researching many spiritual beliefs and religions, I can compare life with a game. A game in which the appearances are illusory like a hologram. It is created to experience, learn, and improve. It is like a program that improves itself. This concept is supported by the fact that as quantum physics demonstrates, our consciousness is affecting the environment around us. We are our own creators as part of this game, we are the contributors to make the game better. The illusion we are living in is perpetuated by our ego, our limitations programming. The ego is not in itself bad as it is programmed to limit our realization that we are in fact part of the main program, the collective consciousness. It is also there to protect our body avatar from destruction, so the experience becomes meaningful. If we do not gentle our ego, we have very few chances to go beyond this limiting survival mode program. The ego is there to give each player an individuality, a myriad of experiences that are then being used to make the program better. The ultimate reward of the detachment from the ego is getting unified with the global consciousness where almost nothing is unknown, and which only becomes richer. Become one with the One Consciousness and you say, "I AM", you say that you are one with God. It is your graduation.

Time as we are perceiving it, as linear and irreversible may be created that way so the consciousness has the opportunity to analyze and learn. As you become one with the global consciousness, time would not matter anymore. It would serve no purpose as all is known; all information is available at once. This information is "stored" and "transmitted" instantly, without any delay, not being limited to the speed of light. Pain and suffering are there to divert us from the early destruction, but also as a learning tool. Pleasure and happiness, even if temporary, is there to give us a glimpse on where we should go and what we should achieve, so they are a learning tool as well. This game is not ending with the winner being the one getting the most coins, having the biggest blocks and so on. The game is never ending, but the reward is the graduation of the soul when it becomes part of the global consciousness. It is where it is fused and effectively disappears in the infinity of it. Until then, the soul is still a player with multiple lives that keeps trying through multiple incarnations. On what it looks like a random choice process, the soul evolves to achieve this infinity. As it learns, it evolves to not be fearful anymore, to realize it is part of the whole and to let anything go and fuse with it, embark on it. I compare it with a drop of water becoming part of the mighty ocean. The drop of water has an existence and goes through "painful" transformations in itself until it becomes part of the ocean. As it becomes part of the ocean, it becomes all knowing, being in direct contact with everything and with no particular locality. Similar to the quantum physics principles, someone observing a drop of water in the ocean sees it only until it does not observe it anymore. Then trying to find it back, it cannot because all drops are the same and there is no individuality. The drop losses itself and transforms itself in something else that can be felt, but it is not visible as a drop anymore. What happens if the drop of water realizes that at one point will become an ocean, so to say that the "resistance is futile" and the "suffering" in between is just a part of the process? It simply goes with the flow, not fearing anything, including death, avoiding "mental suffering" and taking "life" as is with whatever it comes. Does it matter that in the process a drop looks different than other drops of water, it has more numbers attached to it, it is "smarter", it is shinier, larger or of another color? It does not as all will wash away in the mighty infinite, timeless and all-knowing blue ocean.

I hope that I gave you something to think about. Following this analogy, see if you can get your own answer on questions like these:

Does it matter if the water drop becomes part of the ocean faster?

Does it matter if the water drop is poor or rich?

I am sure that you can imagine many other questions for yourself. Dream away and see where this analogy can bring you. See beyond the obvious illusion.

How this statement sounds to you now? - "We are just a drop in the ocean." I would say - "Yes, but we are the Mighty Ocean. We are the Universe!"

And there are not many words I can add to describe what goes next. Go on your path, go on your way, experience it all, enrich us all, become the Ocean, flow through the Universe!

Experience Joy!

Books By This Author

Spirital - A Real Soul Evolution Experience (eBook, Paperback, Hardcover, Audiobook)

Spirital - A Real Soul Evolution Experience, the first volume of the Spirital series is exploring concepts, feelings, realizations, and sensations from a practical perspective, the exact way that Lark experienced them at the time as well as their relation to modern society and the environment. Lark Lauren undergoes a transformation and starts paying attention to the spiritual world, to what is all around us, and to what we take for granted. During the story, the narration changes from the third person to the first person showing the transformation and evolution from the old to the new.

Lark gets us thinking beyond the mainstream and experiencing the deep connection we have with the Universe.

This is a real soul evolution story.

Spirital - Making Sense (eBook, Paperback, Audiobook)

Spirital – Making Sense, the second volume of the Spirital series, is a brainstorming where Lark Lauren is making sense of his experience and associates it with existing and newly created concepts. Lark Lauren puts these concepts and experiences in perspective and in relation to modern society, science, and contemporary challenges. He discusses concepts like awakening, friends, money, business, goals, spirit, books, music, poetry, movies, trends, parallel universes, time, and many more. Even though, these concepts look to be quite different from each other, Lark surprisingly and unexpectedly finds them to be interrelated. Discover what makes and drives them all.

Embark on a journey of auto-discovery and be ready to be wowed by a different perspective. Understand what really means to be happy.

Prepare to be "reborn"!

Spirital - A Real Soul Evolution Experience and Making Sense (Pocketbook Deluxe Edition, Hardcover, Paperback)

This Hardcover Pocketbook Deluxe Edition contains both Volume1 and Volume2 of the Spirital series. Formated in 5.5x8.5in hardcover, and 5x8in paperback to make it easy to take it with you everywhere, for your enjoyment.

A very logical mind, Lark Lauren suffered a traumatic event. He is describing his path to awakening after this event which made him realize there is something else there, beyond the obvious. Follow the inspiring journey that opens him to the truth and puts him on the path of achieving the ultimate Joy.

Spirital - A Real Soul Evolution Experience, the first volume of the Spirital is exploring concepts, feelings, realizations, and sensations from a practical perspective, the exact way that Lark experienced them at the time as well as their relation to modern society and the environment.

Lark Lauren undergoes a transformation and starts paying attention to the spiritual world, to what is all around us, and to what we take for granted. During the story, the narration changes from the third person to the first person showing the transformation and evolution from the old to the new.

Lark gets us thinking beyond the mainstream and experiencing the deep connection we have with the Universe.

This is a real soul evolution story.

Spirital – Making Sense, the second volume of the Spirital series, is a brainstorming where Lark Lauren is making sense of his experience and associates it with existing and newly created concepts. Lark Lauren puts these concepts and experiences in perspective and in relation to modern society, science, and contemporary challenges. He discusses concepts like awakening, friends, money, business, goals, spirit, books, music, poetry, movies, trends, parallel universes, time, and many more. Even though, these concepts look to be quite different from each other, Lark surprisingly and unexpectedly finds them to be interrelated. Discover what makes and drives them all.

Embark on a journey of auto-discovery and be ready to be wowed by a different perspective. Understand what really means to be happy.

Prepare to be "reborn"!

Spirital - The Symphony of Coming Home (eBook, Paperback, Hardcover, Audiobook)

Spirital - The Symphony of Coming Home, the third volume of the Spirital Series, follows the transformation Lark is continuing to experience from the physical and the spiritual perspective.

The book starts with the confirmation that he is on the right path by describing several enlightening visions and continues with the realization that a kundalini force has been awakened in his body. This gives him a wider perspective, allowing him to contemplate his transformation, the world around and ultimately the Universe.

This book essentially describes the findings and beliefs Lark Lauren starts embracing. These become the operating system to function within the spiritual awakening realm, the physical world, and society. The narration moves gradually from the third person at the beginning, when the path is being confirmed, to the first person as the transformation continues and realization settles. Questions that he asks himself are center stage in this process.

Understanding that this state gives him an inclusive, compassionate, and wider perspective, Lark tries something new in the second part of this book. He answers questions that seem to have no answer, questions received from his most avid readers.

Exploring this new perspective reminds us about what is important in life, and what we might be missing.

This book is about nothing and everything at the same time.

Don't miss out!

Visit the website below and you can sign up to receive emails whenever Lark Lauren publishes a new book. There's no charge and no obligation.

https://books2read.com/r/B-A-SRCX-XOAGC

BOOKS 2 READ

Connecting independent readers to independent writers.

About the Author

A very logical mind, Lark suffered a traumatic event. During and after that event, he undergoes a transformation and starts paying attention to the spiritual world, to what is all around us and what we take for granted. He is dedicating the writings in the Spirital series to describe these enlightened experiences, to get us thinking beyond the mainstream and experiencing the deep connection we have with the Universe.